Jay Leno's

HOW TO BE THE FUNNIEST KID IN THE WHOLE WIDE WORLD

(OR JUST IN YOUR CLASS)

ILLUSTRATED BY S. B. WHITEHEAD

Aladdin Paperbacks
New York London Toronto Sydney

To anybody who can't throw a ball and wants to be funny
—J. L.

In memory of Byron Preiss, a man who loved a good joke

Acknowledgments

Special thanks to my comedy partner, Joe Medëiros. We put our two four-year-old minds together and came up with jokes that eight-year-olds would like.

ALADDIN PAPERBACKS
An imprint of Simon & Schuster Children's Publishing Division
1230 Avenue of the Americas, New York, NY 10020
Text copyright © 2005 by Big Dog Productions, Inc.
Illustrations copyright © 2005 by Byron Preiss Visual Publications, Inc., and Big Dog Productions, Inc.
All rights reserved, including the right of reproduction in whole or in part in any form.
ALADDIN PAPERBACKS and related logo are registered trademarks of Simon & Schuster, Inc.
This edition specifically printed for school book fairs by Simon & Schuster.
Also available in a Simon & Schuster Books for Young Readers hardcover edition.
Designed by Red Herring Design
Special thanks to Helga Pollack
The text of this book was set in Clarendon and Trade Gothic.
The illustrations of this book were rendered in watercolor.
Manufactured in the United States of America
First Aladdin Paperbacks edition June 2007
10   9   8   7   6   5   4   3   2   1
The Library of Congress has cataloged the hardcover edition as follows:
Leno, Jay.
Jay Leno's how to be the funniest kid in the whole wide world (or just in your class) / Jay Leno ;
illustrated by S. B. Whitehead.—1st ed.
p. cm.
"A Byron Preiss Visual Productions, Inc. book."
ISBN-13: 978-1-4169-0631-5
ISBN-10: 1-4169-0631-2
1. American wit and humor. I. Whitehead, S. B. II. Title.
PN6165.L46 2005
818'.602—dc22
2005002825
ISBN-13: 978-1-4169-5380-7 (book fair ed.)
ISBN-10: 1-4169-5380-9 (book fair ed.)

TABLE OF CONTENTS

COMEDY 101

I grew up in a small town in New England, which is about as far away geographically from Hollywood as you could get. A lady up the street (who knew no one in Hollywood) told me that the only way to become a successful comedian is if your father is one. The closest my family came to show business was motivational talks my dad would give to inspire the salesmen at the insurance company where he worked. He would play records like Frank Sinatra's *High Hopes* and tell a few jokes. So I assumed that I would not be a comedian but, like my dad, would find another way to be funny.

The first time I made people laugh was an accident. I was just four years old at a gathering of my Italian family. All the women—my aunts, my mother, my girl cousins—were in one room. I ran in and asked a question that had been on my mind for some time. "Aunt Faye," I asked, "why do women have humps like camels?"

There was a huge uproar. Plates dropping, my mother repeating "Oh my goodness, oh my goodness," all the women running around laughing and squealing, *"Did you hear what the boy said?"* And I just stood there confused. "What did I say? What did I say?" As far as I knew, it was a legitimate question. To this day no one's ever answered it.

The first real joke I told was not an accident. In the fourth grade, my friend Joel and I were a comedy team—Jay and Joel. I like to think of this time as my first, ahem, *professional* experience. Well, one day we spent a good part of the morning wrapping Joel in tons of Ace bandages. When he was all wrapped up like a mummy, we put a sign on him that said "10,000 B.C." and wheeled him into the class. Someone asked, "Hey, what do those numbers mean?" I said, "It's the license plate of the truck that hit him." We got a big laugh, followed by a long silence. We didn't have anything else to say.

So my first "professional" joke led to my first professional lesson—you can't rely on props to be funny. Props make it harder, not easier, to move on to your next joke. Also, if you're the wacky guy with the trunk full of props, it's hard to be funny without your trunk full of props. Don't get me wrong—comedians like Carrot Top always make me laugh, but thinking about how much stuff they have to lug around always makes me want to cry, too. But if you can be funny without props, then you can be funny anytime, anywhere, anyhow because you are carrying all the tools of your trade around right in your head. Then if you want to wear a silly hat, it can be just to cover your bad haircut, or distract people from staring at your funny nose or giant chin.

I remember the first time I got a laugh on my own. We were learning about Robin Hood—you know the guy, pointy hat, green tights, robbed from the rich to give to the poor and all that. Anyway, the teacher asked, "Can anyone tell us something about Robin's sidekick Friar Tuck?" I raised my hand. "Friar Tuck was killed by the Sheriff of Nottingham by being boiled in oil." And I quickly added, "Do you know why they boiled him in oil?" My teacher was interested. "No, why?" she asked. I said, "Because he was a friar." Get it? Boiled in oil because he was a fry-er. The whole classroom went hysterical. The teacher finally said, "Okay, stop," but she was laughing too. By the way, I have no idea how Friar Tuck was killed or even if he was killed. But the joke worked, and that was all that mattered to me.

That day I learned two more crucial lessons. Lesson #2: I liked getting laughs; getting laughs made me feel good. And Lesson #3: Making a joke was a lot easier than knowing the real answer!

So here's how to learn to tell jokes. Now remember, it's hard to be funny as a kid because you don't have a lot of life experience to draw on. I mean if you're nine or ten, you've really only been able to stop drooling and pay attention for seven or eight years. So in the beginning, it doesn't hurt to copy someone you like and maybe borrow a real joke or two until you learn how to write your own. I wouldn't advise you to do this for profit or on TV, but just to get a running start.

When I was a kid, I'd watch TV with my mother and I would model myself after whichever comic she found to be funny. Then when I was older, I would play George Carlin's *Class Clown* album over and over and over. He would talk about cutting up in class and the funny things he would do. I would recite his album all the time, at home or in the car, and when I got to the end of his routine, I would add the things that I did as a class clown. Later on, when I first got to do stand-up comedy, I remember waiting to be introduced and doing George's album in my head. I timed it so that when they introduced me I was up to my own part about being a class clown and I would just roll into it on stage.

Once you're comfortable telling other people's jokes, you can start to look around you for your own things to make jokes about—like your parents. What do your parents do that's funny? Follow them around. Does your dad wear funny underwear? Does he wear a silly hat to cover his bad haircut or to distract people from his gigantic chin? Is there something about him that makes you laugh that would make other kids laugh too? Are your neighbors funny? Your pet turtle? Your brothers or sisters? Your mail lady? Your teacher's aide? Your imaginary goat-friend?

Now, once you have the funny stuff, how do you turn it into a joke? There are three things to learn when you want to be a comedian: how to listen, how to talk, and how to be funny. All are very simple.

First, listening. Listen to the people around you; listen closely to how they talk and what they say. Just listen.

Then it's time to learn to talk. Get yourself into situations where you have to talk: at school, in your church or temple, anywhere you're in front of people but not trying to be funny. The best way to do this is by introducing someone: "Ladies and gentlemen, please welcome Rabbi So-and-so." In a situation like that, there's no pressure on you to be funny. You're just learning to talk in front of a group. When you see all those faces looking at you, you might feel a little anxiety. If someone distracts you by coughing, you might forget what you were going to say. It's okay to mess up; just keep doing it.

When you're comfortable with groups, go a step further. If your school or church has a talent show, ask if you can be the Master of Ceremonies, the person who introduces the acts. "Please welcome Little Billy and his dancing poodle, Rocky." If you are comfortable, you might be able to add a little joke to the introductions. If it gets a laugh, keep going. If it doesn't, move on, introduce the next act, and try again later. But just keep going.

Now that you can listen and talk, let's turn to being funny. The hardest thing for you to determine is the first five minutes of material for your act, because whatever you do in your first five minutes really defines you. It sets the tone for the kind of comedy you like. I've found that the real trick of finding material is to take stories from my life and turn them into jokes.

When I started as a comedian, I would memorize jokes and simply go on stage and tell them. Then after the show I'd sit at a restaurant with the other comedians and we would talk and tell funny stories about awful places we'd worked at or shows that went bad. I was telling one of these stories one night and someone said, "You know, you should tell that on stage." I said, "But it doesn't have a beginning or an end." He said, "Yeah, but when the story's funny, it doesn't have to have a beginning and an end." Then I went on stage and did it and it worked really well. It was a turning point. I started taking stories from my life, especially about my parents, and turning it into material. I also realized that no one could steal my act because it was about me and my family, and so in some ways it was also good protection.

Family is a good source for material and so are you. Comedy can come from imperfections. A very famous comedy team the Smothers Brothers began as a folk singing duo, just two brothers named Dick and Tommy. Tommy is dyslexic, and so he would read the words to the songs and when he would get them wrong, they started getting laughs. So, they began to exaggerate his confusion for laughs and they went on to be big stars! If you have some perceived imperfection, use it! If you're short, do short jokes. Find something about yourself that other people think is odd or that you think is odd. Be willing to risk being laughed at. "I'm not on the team because I'm so slow . . ."

M ost comedians tend to be a bit different from other people—smaller, or fatter, or taller, or geekier. If you have one of these characteristics, it might actually help you to have a career in comedy. If you're the handsomest boy or prettiest girl in your class, it's going to be a tougher road.

Another thing to realize is that you do not have to use cuss words to be funny. It's not that you shock or offend with the words, but using them shows a lack of imagination. I find it more challenging and often funnier to find less common descriptions. For example, rather than saying someone's fat, I might say they are big-boned or heavyset. Also, by having clean material, you will appeal to the widest audience possible.

So, okay, you have your material. Now what? Practice. Practice, practice, and practice more. The best thing to do is to tape-record yourself. I used to record my act and then take the laughs off of a Don Rickles album to give it some authenticity. My joke, his laughs. And you have to repeat yourself. Everyone knows that the way to get better at anything is to keep doing it—and that includes storytelling. If you tell a funny story early in the day, keep retelling it and by the last class you've got it refined. Think about what you added or took out that made it funnier.

You can be really funny, but if you have stage fright, you have to determine where it starts and learn to combat it. One trick is to practice on an empty stage. When I was seventeen or eighteen years old, I washed dishes at a popular night club in Boston. I thought being around professional comedians would help me break into the industry. After work, when I was done and the show was over, I'd go up on the empty stage and just tell my stories, just to see what it felt like—people would come later.

W hen it is time to practice in front of people, don't use your family. Never perform for your family. They either laugh too hard or not at all. Comedy is the only profession where love from a stranger is better than love from a family member. You need to perform for strangers to see if you're really funny. If they laugh and cheer, it's the greatest thing in the world. Having a great show and getting laughs is like being in a mosh pit. The crowd keeps you up. You just float over them.

If you still want to be a comedian, this book can help. Besides having hundreds of jokes, there are great tips scattered throughout. Remember, though, this book is not school, it's comedy. It's supposed to be fun. And humor can bring people together. To see what a difference a crowd makes to your jokes, try watching a funny movie at a movie theater, and then go home and watch it alone. It probably won't seem nearly as funny to you. There's nothing infectious about laughing alone. It's the same as storytelling around a campfire: You need the people. Comedy brings people together. You can't do it at home sending text messages. So get out there and make them laugh.

Where does the Army keep fish?

In a tank.

What do you call a blind horse?

Can't Seebiscuit.

What kind of math can you teach to cows?

Cow-culus.

What's the most agile type of bat?

An acrobat.

What's a lion's favorite state?

Maine.

How can you tell when a camel is from Beverly Hills?

Because there's silicone in its humps.

Two birds were at the ocean when one of them got caught in an oil spill. The bird in the oil spill could eat, but the other one went hungry. Why?

The oily bird gets the worm.

Why did the turtle take assertiveness training?
He wanted to come out of his shell.

What's the coldest place an ant can go?
The Antarctic.

A pig fell into a meat grinder. It brought out the wurst in him.

AMAZING
animals

Why is it easy to fool sheep?
Because you can always pull the wool over their eyes.

Of what political persuasion are sheep?
They're bleating-heart liberals.

How do whales cry?
They blubber.

Why are there no zebras in Scotland?
Because stripes clash with plaids.

How do turkeys eat?

They gobble their food.

What kind of bull do you find in turkey?

Istanbul.

How do you get a cow to get out of the way?

Just say, "Moo-ve."

Why don't ostriches fly?

They can't get past airline security.

What type of bat likes to fight?

A combat.

What is the craziest animal in the zoo?

A bi-polar bear.

Why can you never trust the fastest
animal in the world?
Because he's a cheetah.

How do you get a horse's attention?
Just yell, "Hey!"

What type of bee
is the smartest?
A spelling bee.

What's a crowbar?
It's where crows drink.

What's a bear's
ancestor called?
A forebear.

Judy: Have you ever seen an antelope?
Trudy: No, all my aunts had church weddings.

ZANIEST SOUNDING WORDS

squat ★ festoonery ★ ectosarc ★ kiskadee ★ vicissitude ★
tootsy ★ zax ★ gynantherous ★ dropsy ★
befuddled ★ jejune

WHAT TIME DO DUCKS WAKE UP?

At the quack
of dawn.

9

STRANGEST BODY NOISES

sneezes ★ gurgles ★ gulps ★
hiccups ★ burps ★
farts ★ stomach rumbles

Out of all the animals, why is the rabbit the coolest?

Because it can hip-hop.

What do you call a parrot when it flies away?

A polygon.

What do ants take for an upset stomach?

An antacid.

When is down up?

When a duck is in flight.

Where do ants live?

Usually with uncles.

What kind of bull is easily fooled?

A gulli-bull.

10

What goes "fweet, fweet, fweet"?
A bird with a mouth full of crackers.

What happened to the dog who fell in the freezer?

He became a frozen pupsicle.

Why do horses wear blinders?
So they don't become sea horses.

What's the main difference between a duck and George Washington?

One has a bill on his face, the other his face on a bill.

What kind of bug only comes out at Christmastime?
A humbug.

11

What's a billy goat's baby called?
Billy the Kid.

What do you give a buffalo
when he's done
eating his dinner?
The Buffalo Bill.

What swims in water, is big and white
and goes "quack, quack"?
Moby Duck.

Why was the African tribesman happy that
his herd of gnus was stolen?
Because no gnus is good gnus.

What kind of tile
would you never
want to find in your
bathroom?
A reptile.

What's black and white and
red all over?
A polar bear with an infected tattoo.

Why did the teacher at the obedience school make the dog sit in the corner?

Because he was bad to the bone.

Who's the most famous singing sheep?

Baa-baa Streisand.

Why wasn't the park ranger upset when he saw an injured owl?

Because he knew that time heals owl wounds.

What happens to frogs when they're angry?

They get hopping mad.

What kind of moose tastes best?

Chocolate moose.

13

Where do cows go on vacation?

Cowlifornia.

**Did you hear about the chicken that got
in trouble with the police?**

She ran afowl of the law.

**Why did the horse
leave his wife?**

She was a nag.

**What do you get when you
burn wood that's been
eaten by termites?**

Holey smoke.

**What part of your
body is most
like a baby animal?**

Your calf.

How do amoebas talk to each other?

By cell phone.

**What did the gopher say when
he lost all his money?**

"Gopher broke."

What animal says "mooski"?

A Moscow.

What do you call a boat full of fish eggs?

A roeboat.

How do you fix an injured duck?

With duct tape!

Where do worms play baseball?

Wriggly Field.

What's a sheep's favorite music group?

Ewe-2.

What are the easiest animals to weigh?

Fish, because they have scales.

ASK JAY

HOW DO YOU START BUILDING A ROUTINE?

Always keep a tape recorder or pen and paper nearby. If you jot down ten things during the day and one ends up being truly funny, you are doing better than most comedians. A very small percentage of the jokes I write make it into my act. So take a routine one joke at a time. If one joke doesn't work, drop it and move on to the next. Soon you'll find what you thought was your funniest material is now your least funny. That's a sign that you are getting a better routine.

QUESTION: Have you ever taken One-A-Day vitamins?

IRON JAY: No, I never knew how many to take.

ASK IRON JAY

Iron Jay is a health and fitness expert. He's spent a lot more time developing his body than he has developing his mind.

QUESTION: Iron Jay, how can I avoid getting water on the knee?

IRON JAY: I'd say don't kneel down where it's wet.

QUESTION: How much sleep should a person get?

IRON JAY: I say a person should have at least eight hours of sleep a day and even more at night.

QUESTION: How can I tone up my gluteus maximus?
IRON JAY: I have a Nissan Maxima and I usually just change the spark plugs every 20,000 miles.

QUESTION: Do you like fat-free products?

IRON JAY: If the fat don't cost extra, I say take it.

QUESTION: Iron Jay, is it possible for dogs to get bigger through exercise?

IRON JAY: Yes it is. I know a dog that started as a miniature poodle and ended up a husky.

17

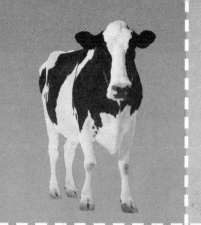

QUESTION: Where do they get nonfat milk?

MR. BRAIN: Skinny cows.

QUESTION: Have you seen STAR WARS?

MR. BRAIN: Seen it? I was supposed to play Darth Vader.

QUESTION: Why didn't you get the part?

MR. BRAIN: The stupid helmet wouldn't fit over my head.

QUESTION: What is the purpose of the asteroid belt?

MR. BRAIN: To hold up the asteroid's pants.

QUESTION: They say that the universe is expanding. Why is that?

MR. BRAIN: The universe must expand to make room for all those Starbucks stores they keep opening up.

ASK Mr. BRAIN

**Mr. Brain is the smartest man in the world.
But unfortunately, he has no people skills.
So forgive him if his answers are a bit rude.**

QUESTION: I have a bad case of dandruff. Is there anything you recommend?

MR. BRAIN: Yes, a hat.

What do you call someone who won't spend money on a Jeep?
A Jeepskate.

What's a Norwegian's favorite type of car?
A fjord.

Is it true that if you take a corner too fast, a Mercedes-Benz?

CA

SILLY SPORTS

curling ★ thumb wrestling ★ cockroach racing ★
hand fishing ★ bylong mouse racing ★ coal carrying
★ tossing the caber ★ cup stacking

If some new cars have satellite radio, what kinds of cars have cable?

Cable cars.

21

CATS & dogs

What happened to the kitten that got caught in the Xerox machine?

He became a copycat.

Which of Shakespeare's plays is about a dog?

Hamlet, because he was a great Dane.

Did you hear about the dog that was so high-strung, he developed a nervous tick?

Do we have any dog owners in the audience? Can I see a show of paws?

**I had a dog that was so lazy, he had a prerecorded bark.
He was so lazy, he used to chase parked cars.
The only thing he could do well was play dead.
In fact, he was so good, I buried him three times.**

FUNNIEST-SOUNDING DOG BREEDS

Shih tzu ★ Affenpinscher ★ Ainu Dog ★ Bergamasco ★ Alaskan Klee Kai ★ Beauceron ★ Yorkipoo ★ Dandie Dinmont Terrier ★ Goldendoodle ★ Leonberger ★ Spinone Italiano ★ Bouvier des Flandres

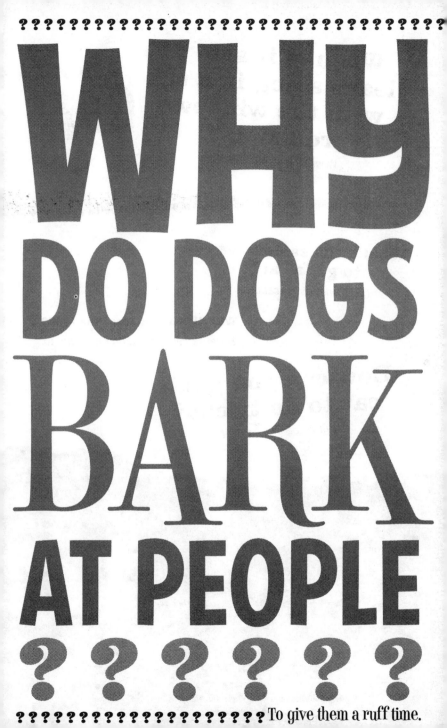

? ?

WHY
DO DOGS
BARK
AT PEOPLE
? ? ? ? ? ?

? To give them a ruff time.

When is it safe to leave a dog in a car with the windows rolled up?

When he's in a convertible.

What's a cat's favorite country?
Purr-u.

What's the easiest way to get a cat?
Order one from a catalog.

Why did the cat cross the road?
Because her owner didn't want her to.

How can you get a cat to do tricks?
Put a dog in a cat suit.

What's a cat's favorite color?

Purr-ple.

What musical note do you hear when a car runs over a bee?

Bee-flat.

What do you get when you take a gene from a parrot and put it into a cat?

You get a cat that can speak but has no interest in talking to you.

Why do dogs like trees so much?

They're attracted to the bark.

Criss cross

What do you get when you cross a suitcase with the Bible?

Samsonite and Delilah.

What do you get when you cross a lightbulb with a baby?

A lightbulb that cries when it needs to be changed.

Why did the horse trainer cross a thoroughbred with an elephant?

So he'd get a horse that would always win by a nose.

What kind of food do you get when you cross Lassie and a chrysanthemum?

Collie-flower.

What did the farmer get when he crossed a cow and a duck?

Cheese and quackers.

Why did the farmer cross a chicken with a centipede?

He wanted a bird with a hundred drumsticks.

DAFFY

Definitions

GOING AGAINST THE GRAIN:

Being on a no-carb diet.

EMINEM:

A candy rapper.

MICROCHIPS:

Those crumbs in the bottom of a Ruffles bag.

AN OCTAGON:

A square that someone cut corners on.

EMIT:

Something worn by a baseball catcher.

Did you hear about the dummy who sent his Dalmatian to the dry cleaners?

They removed its spots.

Why did the dummy put a fir tree in his living room?

He wanted to spruce up the place.

Why did the dummy take the stairs to the 99th floor?

He wanted to come up the hard way.

Why did the dummy fire a gun up the chimney?

He wanted his flue shot.

Why did the dummy throw his paycheck in the trash?

He wanted to have disposable income.

Why did the dumb fisherman bait his hook with plutonium?

For nuclear fission.

Dummy
jokes

Why did the dummy throw oranges into the ocean?

Because they were naval oranges.

DID YOU HEAR ABOUT THE DUMMY WHO GOT ALL OUT OF BREATH FROM BLOWING THE LEAVES OFF HIS

SIDEWALK?

ASK JAY

DO YOU HAVE ANY TRICKS TO COMBAT STAGE FRIGHT?

When I was a little kid, I used to wear glasses. I would take them off before I walked up on stage so that everyone in the audience looked a little blurry. I could hear people react, but I couldn't see if someone was frowning, so it wouldn't throw me. Another way to combat stage fright is to look at the spotlight while performing. Later you can learn how to make eye contact, but first you need to learn to work through the fear.

31

Why did the dummy launch his Christmas tree?

Because he wanted to see the fir fly.

Why did the dummy drink a gallon of water before every meal?

So he could whet his appetite.

Why did the dummy give his father a couple of lazy men for Christmas?

Because his dad wanted a pair of loafers.

Why did the dummy throw a can of soup and a can of beans?

He wanted to see toucans fly.

Why did the dummy blow into a bunch of faucets?

He was trying to play taps.

WELCOME TO Smileyberg "Have a nice day"

GOOFIEST TOWNS IN AMERICA

Cheesequake, New Jersey ★ Monkey's Eyebrow, Arizona ★ Hygiene, Colorado ★ Yeehaw Junction, Florida ★ Santa Claus, Indiana ★ Beebeetown, Iowa ★ Smileyberg, Kansas ★ Shoulderblade, Kentucky ★ Hot Coffee, Mississippi ★ Pumpkin Center, Missouri ★ Truth or Consequences, New Mexico ★ Chocolate Bayou, Texas ★ Humptulips, Washington

Why did the dummy invent a polygraph machine for puppies?

He couldn't let sleeping dogs lie.

Why did the dummy spray his computer with Raid?

He was trying to debug it.

Why did the dummy put a chicken in a flowerpot?

He wanted eggplant.

Why did the dummy smell a dollar bill?

So he could tell how many scents were in it.

Why was the dummy thrown out of the seafood restaurant?

He kept trying to feel everyone's mussels.

33

Why did the dummy throw a playing card down a mine shaft?

Because he wanted to have an ace in the hole.

Why did the dumb farmer take a bath in the back of the cornfield?

His mother always told him to wash behind his ears.

Did you hear about the dummy who was eager to go fishing?

He waited by the lake with bated breath.

Why did the dummy take a bread roll to the fashion show?

He wanted it to be a roll model.

Why did the dummy refuse to pay the tailor for ironing his pants?

Because he thinks the Constitution guarantees the right to a free press.

Why did the dummy throw an apple into the air?

He wanted to see a fruit fly.

Why did the dummy put salt and pepper all over his Christmas cards?

He wanted to send seasoned greetings.

Did you hear about the dummy who put a dozen sheep in his Christmas tree?

Instead of flocking his tree, he was treeing his flock.

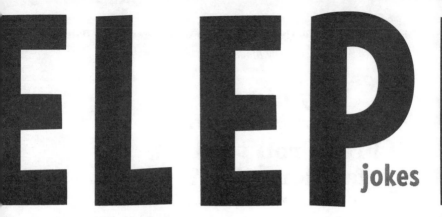

ELEP

jokes

How can you tell when an elephant is owned by a mobster?

There's a dead body in the trunk.

Why do elephants go swimming?

To get their trunks wet.

Who's the most famous elephant jazz singer?

Elephants Gerald.

Why can't an elephant ever be on the radio?

He would break it.

Why do you never find elephants in cold weather?

Because they don't make earmuffs that fit them.

How can you get a female elephant into a size 9 dress?

By telling her it's a size 6.

Why did the elephant cross the road?

He was filling in for the chicken.

36

Why won't you ever see an elephant on an airplane?

Because the last time one of them flew, the airline lost his trunk.

Eskimos

**What do Eskimos use
to build their houses?**

Iglue.

**GIRL: Is it true that chafing
is the biggest problem facing
Eskimos who kiss by
rubbing noses?
GUY: No, it's snot.**

**Did you hear about the Eskimo girl
who knew her boyfriend was cheating
because she found another woman's
nose hair on his collar?**

What kind of cereal do Eskimos eat?

Mush!

Where do Eskimos keep their money?

In a snowbank.

TEN THINGS
NOT TO DO TO THE FAMILY PET

make your cats have a tea party ★ dress your dog as a superhero ★
make your parrot wear sombreros ★ let your fish drive the car ★
teach your hamster to do the Macarena ★ put your gerbil in your
sister's mitten ★ wear your iguana as a scarf ★ name your bunny Rover
★ put lipstick on your monkey ★ feed any pet to your pet snake

Why can you never fool a baby on the day he was born?

Because he wasn't born yesterday.

Why are a grandfather's teeth like the stars?

Because they come out at night.

What's the best way not to fight with your little brother?

Don't unlock the closet you put him in.

What holiday is devoted to women who have had babies? Mother's Day?

No, Labor Day.

Why do mothers put so much powder on their babies?

Talc is cheap.

It's a wise old proverb that says: A boy who lets his uncle's wives wear his jeans will have aunts in his pants.

Woman: My daughter and her boyfriend are getting pretty serious. The other day they exchanged rings. She gave him the one in her nose. He gave her the one in his lip.

**What would you get if
you cloned Cher?**

Cher and Cher-alike.

**Why did the Dalai
Lama go to Las Vegas?**

He wanted Tibet.

FAMOUS
& FICTIONAL
People

**What would you get if you cloned
Bishop Tutu?**

Bishop Tutu and Bishop Tutu-too.

Why are England's Prince Harry and Prince William always together?

Because you shouldn't split heirs.

What does a supermodel call a can of peas?

An all-you-can-eat buffet.

What did Isaac Newton say when the apple fell on his head?

Ouch.

How do you know that Edgar Allan Poe didn't have money?

Because he lived in the Poe house.

Why did Jack-Be-Nimble stop jumping over the candlestick and start jumping over chimes?

He wanted to be a bellhop.

What's it called when people talk about Kelly Clarkson, Clay Aiken, and Ruben Studdard?

Idol chitchat.

Why are LAWYERS never upset when they get an affidavit ?

Because affidavit's better than no davit at all.

Snoop Dogg had a birthday today. When asked what it was like to get older, Snoop said, "Ruff."

What happened when Sigmund Freud went for a walk on a frozen pond?

He discovered the Freudian slip.

What would have happened if the witch had eaten Hansel and Gretel?

She'd have invented the first Kid's Meal.

What was the skinniest part of Emperor Napoléon?

The bony part.

How does Santa Claus fire an elf?

He gives him the old heave-ho-ho-ho.

Why does Superman fly all the way to South Africa to get his clothes?

Because that's where Cape Town is.

Why was Sir Lancelot tired all the time?

Because he worked the knight shift.

Why did the supermodel cross the road?

Because there was a mirror on the other side.

Where did the
Three Little Pigs
get

MO

to build
their houses?

NEY

From a piggy bank.

FOOD

What's the heaviest soup you can get?

Wonton.

Why doesn't the warden ever give prisoners chocolate?

It'll make them break out.

What do you call someone who hates salad?

Antipasto.

What type of fruit has a built-in bed?

An apricot.

If you get sushi in Japanese restaurants and chow mein in Chinese restaurants, what do you get in Korean restaurants?

Seoul food.

What do you get when you put glue in your oatmeal?

A breakfast that sticks to your ribs.

What fruit will never run away and get married?

A cantaloupe.

ASK JAY

DID YOU HAVE AN AFTER-SCHOOL JOB?

All through high school, I worked at McDonald's. Believe it or not, my job flipping burgers was responsible for my career in comedy. McDonald's put on a regional talent show. My manager suggested I put together a comedy routine for the show. So I got together with a guy named Jay Monroe and came up with a routine. We won the competition and the $150 cash prize. That was the first glimmer that I could make money by telling jokes. All thanks to McDonald's.

Did you hear about the waffle that
was run over by a truck?
It was as flat as a pancake.

How do you
scramble an egg?

Like this: ne gag.

Why did the new cook at the Army base bring
one thousand hot dogs into the barracks at 5 a.m.?
Because he heard that every morning, the soldiers were mustered.

What kind of mint is deadly if thrown?
Spearmint.

What's a gardener's favorite dessert?
Pie à la mowed.

What's the best way to serve Brussels sprouts?

With a tennis racket.

What's the most popular restaurant at the North Pole?
Brr-grr King.

What's the hardest thing about making shoofly pie?
Putting shoes on the flies.

Why is the

BANANA
so popular?

Because it has appeal.

What do you call cheese that's not yours?

Nacho cheese.

What do you call someone who completely destroys a box of Cap'n Crunch?

A cereal killer.

Why aren't there any restaurants in outer space?

Because there's no atmosphere.

What does Homer Simpson use to make bread?

D'oh!

Why do doors sometimes stick?

Because of the door jam.

What do you call an Oreo that has computer chips in it?

A smart cookie.

CAFETERIA

LUNCHES TO SKIP

mystery meat ★ spam soufflé ★
anchovy cupcakes ★ creamed chipped trout ★
Jell-O cubes with bits o' ham ★
kidney surprise ★ nostril nuggets ★
liver loaf

**How do astronauts make Chinese
food in outer space?**

They take a space wok.

**Did you hear about the
manic-depressive who brought
cherry pies to the bowling alley?**

He was a bipolar pie bowler.

**Italians always have food
on their minds. Even when
they're saying good-bye,
they say "Chow."**

**If you use paper plates at a picnic, what
kind of plates do you use indoors?**

Indochina.

55

Where would you go to see a pole vault? The Olympics?

No, a bank in Warsaw.

What country of Africa is made up of two bars of soap?

Ivory Coast.

GEOGRAPHY

What is the English Channel?

The BBC.

How do you make a Belgian waffle?

Ask him to make a really tough decision.

What's the best-smelling city in the world?

Cologne, Germany.

How long is the Great Wall of China?

From beginning to end.

What do people in India write on their postcards?

"Having a wonderful time. Vishnu were here."

What country is always out of breath?

Iran.

What do you call someone in Asia who's under 21?

Asia Minor.

In France,
if someone pretends
to be your father,
what is he called?

A faux pas.

What kind of electricity
do they use in Israel?

Israelites.

58

What do people in Panama wish each other
during the holidays?

Merry Isthmus.

A man from the Czech Republic wanted to go to America but couldn't afford the airfare. So he put himself in a box and posted himself from Prague. This is how we got the phrase:

"The Czech is in the mail."

In what state do you find the smallest soft drink?

Minnesota.

ODDEST MUSEUMS

The Condiment Packet Museum
The Potato Museum
Rome's National Pasta Museum
Museum of Dentistry
Marvin Johnson's Gourd Museum
Museum of Questionable Medical Devices
International Museum of Surgical Science
Porter Thermometer Museum
Merry-Go-Round Museum
Bata Shoe Museum
Sixth Floor Museum
American Museum of Fly Fishing
Nutcracker Museum
Honey of a Museum
Kansas Oil Museum and Hall of Fame

Which Great Lake thinks it's better than all the others?

Lake Superior.

HARE-BRAINED

What do you use to comb a rabbit?

A harebrush.

What would happen if rabbits could drive cars?

We'd have hare pollution.

Boy: My rabbit ran away!
Girl: You know what they say:
Hare today, gone tomorrow.

Why did the dummy keep a rabbit on his face?

He wanted facial hare.

What do you get when you cross a heart surgeon with a rabbit?

A hare transplant.

Lily: I just went into my brother's room.
Why does he have a baby rabbit on his bureau?

Mother: Well, your brother's a teenager now and he
wants a little hare on his chest.

JAY'S
FUNNY FRIENDS

GEORGE CARLIN—Class Clown, Hippy Dippy Weatherman

"AMERICA THE BEAUTIFUL" LYRICS
O beautiful for smoggy skies
Insecticided grains
For strip-mined mountains, majesty
Above the asphalt plain.
America, America,
Man sheds his waste on thee
And hides the pines
With billboard signs
From sea to oily sea!

ABBOTT AND COSTELLO—"WHO'S ON FIRST" EXCERPT

BUD: I'm telling you: Who's on first, What's on second,
I Don't Know is on third.
LOU: You know the fellows' names?
BUD: Yes.
LOU: Well, then, who's playin' first?
BUD: Yes.
LOU: I mean the fellow's name on first base.
BUD: Who.
LOU: The fellow playin' first base for St. Louis.
BUD: Who.
LOU: The guy on first base.
BUD: Who is on first.
LOU: Well what are you askin' me for?
BUD: I'm not asking you—I'm telling you:
Who is on first.

61

HISTORY

When were the Dark Ages?
Before lightbulb jokes were invented.

When did the Stone Age begin?
When Mick Jagger was born.

Where was the Declaration of Independence signed?
At the bottom.

True or false: George Washington's teeth?
They were false.

What's a Pilgrim's favorite country?
Turkey.

When can you find a knight's belly button?
In the middle of the knight.

How were peasants awakened in the Middle Ages?
By someone yelling, "Serfs up!"

What kind of music did the Pilgrims listen to?
Plymouth Rock.

Why did Cain kill his brother?
Because he was Abel.

Which adverb surrendered to General Grant at Appomattox?
Generally.

62

**Ben Franklin: What kind of a job did
Betsy Ross do on the flag?**
George Washington: Sew-sew.

ASK JAY

HOW DO YOU STOP SOMEONE WHO IS HECKLING YOU?

When you are a kid, you probably won't get heckled. But as you get older, it happens, so you should be prepared. Over the years I've learned that you shouldn't ignore it but deal with it quickly. If I'm on stage and someone yells at me, I'll stop the show and say, "Yes, sir. What's your question?" When all of the attention is on him, a heckler will usually get stage fright. Also, unless he has been practicing for this moment, he probably won't be funnier than you. If he responds with something like "I think you stink," the audience will usually side with you because you've dealt with the problem. You can then say, "Maybe you have a funnier joke; let's hear your joke." That usually shuts a heckler down and you can go on with your routine.

Knock
Knock
jokes

KNOCK, KNOCK.
Who's there?
Hugo.
Hugo who?
Hugo girl!

KNOCK, KNOCK.
Who's there?
Scotland.
Scotland who?
Scotland me 5 bucks.

KNOCK, KNOCK.
Who's there?
Justin.
Justin who?
Justin time for dinner.

KNOCK, KNOCK.
Who's there?
Izzy.
Izzy who?
Izzy home?

KNOCK, KNOCK.
Who's there?
Denise.
Denise who?
Denise and de
nephew are at the door.

KNOCK, KNOCK.
Who's there?
Lisa.
Lisa who?
Lisa new car at
Big Jay's Motors.

KNOCK, KNOCK.
Who's there?
Armageddon.
Armageddon who?
Armageddon a new
bicycle for my birthday?

Knock, knock.

Who's there?

TUR

Turnip who?

Turnip the heat. It's freezing in here.

NIP.

KNOCK, KNOCK.
Who's there?
Ya.
Ya who?
What's all the cheering about?

KNOCK, KNOCK.
Who's there?
Ava.
Ava who?
Ava been around here before?

KNOCK, KNOCK.
Who's there?
Euripides.
Euripides who?
Euripides pants and
you won't get
another pair.

KNOCK, KNOCK.
Who's there?
Ida.
Ida who?
Ida rather you not
come knocking at
this time of day.

KNOCK, KNOCK.
Who's there?
Joe.
Joe who?
Joe mama.

KNOCK, KNOCK.
Who's there?
Andrew.
Andrew who?
Andrew a really nice picture of me.

KNOCK, KNOCK.
Who's there?
Colin.
Colin who?
Colin sick to
work today and
we'll go out.

KNOCK, KNOCK.
Who's there?
Hanoi.
Hanoi who?
Hanoi someone else
for a change.

KNOCK, KNOCK.
Who's there?
Samoa.
Samoa who?
Samoa kids are coming over to play.

KNOCK, KNOCK.
Who's there?
Jamaican.
Jamaican who?
Jamaican steak or chicken for dinner?

KNOCK, KNOCK.
Who's there?
Sudan.
Sudan who?
Sudan in court if he won't pay
the money he owes you.

KNOCK, KNOCK.
Who's there?
Taiwan.
Taiwan who?
Taiwan knot in this string.

ten most RIDICULOUS NAMES

Paige Turner ★ Ann Chovie ★ Betty Didditt ★ Carrie Oakey ★ Dora Jarre ★
Ella Vator ★ Frieda Livery ★ Isabelle Ringing ★ Justin Time ★ Oliver Suddin

69

KNOCK, KNOCK.

Who's there? Wayne.

Wayne who?

Wayne's expected later today
so BWING an umbrella.

KNOCK, KNOCK.
Who's there?
Atch.
Atch who?
Gesundheit.

KNOCK, KNOCK.
Who's there?
Alpaca.
Alpaca who?
Alpaca sweater because
it's going to be cold.

KNOCK, KNOCK.
Who's there?
Noah.
Noah who?
Noah body home.

KNOCK, KNOCK.
Who's there?
Caesar.
Caesar who?
Caesar before she gets away.

KNOCK, KNOCK.
Who's there?
Snow.
Snow who?
Snow body home.

KNOCK, KNOCK.
Who's there?
Cook.
Cook who?
Cuckoo for Cocoa Puffs.

KNOCK, KNOCK.
Who's there?
Lettuce.
Lettuce who?
Lettuce stop doing these knock knock jokes.

Teacher: Jay, define this word: INTENSE.
Li'l Jay: Where Boy Scouts sleep.

Li'l Jay: I wanted to do something special for my mom's birthday. So I gift-wrapped the wash.

Louie: Jay, what are you reading?
Li'l Jay: A book on attention deficit disorder.
Louie: How is it?
Li'l Jay: I don't know. I can't get past the first page.

Teacher: Use the word DECRIMINALIZE in a sentence.
Li'l Jay: You could tell he was a thief. He had decriminalize.

Teacher: If Johnny had three apples and Timmy had five apples, what would you have?
Li'l Jay: A computer lab.

Teacher: In WWII, who did the Czechs clash with?
Li'l Jay: The plaids.

Teacher: How long did the Iron Age last?
Li'l Jay: Until they invented permanent press.

Teacher: Jay, where will you usually find whales—and don't tell me in Wales.
Li'l Jay: All right, Finland.

Camp Counselor: Jay, would you like to toast a marshmallow?
Li'l Jay: Sure! Here's to you, marshmallow!

REASONS
TO STAY HOME SICK
bad haircutitis ★ test todaycinosis ★
gym classaphobia ★ unexpected zits
syndrome ★ putrid lunch allergy ★
mean kid measles ★ report due flu ★
daytime TV watchis

Girl: Brown eyes run in my family.
Li'l Jay: Noses run in mine.

75

Teacher: Jay, how do you get a square root?

Li'l Jay: Put a tree in a square pot.

Teacher: Jay, give me the definition of procrastination.

Li'l Jay: I'll do it later.

Teacher: Now, who can explain Einstein's Theory of Relativity?

Li'l Jay: Einstein?

Uncle: Hey, there are only fifty-one cards in this deck. Where's the missing one?

Li'l Jay: It got lost in the shuffle.

Louie: Why is your dad so mad?

Li'l Jay: Because my dog ate scraps.

Louie: You shouldn't feed him from the table.

Li'l Jay: I didn't. Scraps is the neighbor's cat.

Friend: My friend Juan comes from a big family, but I've never met any of them.

Li'l Jay: It doesn't matter. When you've seen Juan, you've seen them all.

Teacher: What's a light-year?

Li'l Jay: A year when you don't have much to do.

Teacher: What's the difference between Hepatitis A and Hepatitis B?

Li'l Jay: One letter.

Teacher: Jay, can you describe what a walnut is?

Li'l Jay: That's it in a nutshell.

Teacher: Use the word MOTIF in a sentence.

Li'l Jay: My grandma wears dentures because she has no motif.

Teacher: Jay, what's "Eureka"?

Li'l Jay: It's Italian for "You need deodorant."

Teacher: What is a psychopath?

Li'l Jay: Where crazy people jog.

Teacher: Jay, what is zinc?

Li'l Jay: The present tense of zunk.

Teacher: Jay, what's amnesia?

Li'l Jay: I forget.

Teacher: Who said, "I cannot tell a lie"?

Li'l Jay: Not sure, but I know it wasn't a lawyer.

Teacher: What's "illegal"?

Li'l Jay: It's a sick bird.

Teacher: What did Thomas Edison mean when he said, "Genius is 1 percent inspiration and 99 percent perspiration"?

Li'l Jay: That geniuses don't smell so good.

Teacher: Jay, what is a boycott?

Li'l Jay: Something else a Boy Scout sleeps on.

Teacher: Define "royalty."

Li'l Jay: A queen's favorite drink.

Teacher: What is a subordinate clause?

Li'l Jay: Someone who works under Santa.

Teacher: Jay, what are taste buds?

Li'l Jay: The answer's right on the tip of my tongue.

Li'l Jay: Keep saying the word "our" until I tell you to stop.

Girl: Our, our, our, our, our, our, our, our, our, our—

Li'l Jay: Stop.

Girl: Why did you stop me then?

Li'l Jay: I was waiting till the eleventh our.

Girl: Can you use the words *account, afford, attire, attack, aboard,* and *abridge* in a sentence?

Li'l Jay: Sure. Account drove afford over abridge, ran over aboard with attack in it and blew attire.

Teacher: Name a unit of electrical energy.

Li'l Jay: What?

Teacher: That's correct.

There was a young man with no brain.
When it stormed, his head filled with rain.
But this poor dumb fellah
Didn't buy an umbrella.
Instead he just put in a drain.

Lime

There was a young girl who ate mice,
Tin cans, old shoes, and dead lice.
She'd go out on a date
And she'd eat what she ate
And never get asked somewhere twice.

There was a young man named Drew,
Who weighed in at three-thirty-two.
He was in love with a skater
And he wanted to date her,
But in breaking the ice, he fell through.

General Custer thought he had luck,
But at Little Big Horn the Indians struck.
Of pride he was full
Till he met Sitting Bull
And ended up a Sitting Duck.

icks

There was a gourmet named Billy
Who dined from Beijing to Philly.
His only complaint
About the places he ate
Was that the chili in Chile was chilly.

There once was a bald man named Hugh.
On his head he got a tattoo.
But instead of black ink,
He used chartreuse and pink.
Now Hugh is a horrible hue.

FAVORITE
WAYS TO DRIVE SIBLINGS CRAZY

repeat everything they say ★ tickle them until they throw up ★
poke them repeatedly in the forehead ★ make notes in their diaries ★
blast the radio to heavy metal while they're doing their homework ★
pick up the phone while they're on and make zoo animal noises ★
draw glasses on their school photos

Medical Marvels

Why is the blood in your body always sad?
Because no matter what it does, it always ends up in defeat.

Four out of five doctors agree— the fifth doctor is an idiot.

Johnson cut his hand working in the backyard and went to the hospital.

"You'll need three stitches," said the young doctor, who was just out of medical school.

"Well, I'm not letting you do it," said Johnson.

"Fine," said the doctor. "Suture self."

What does an embryo do when it's hungry?

It calls womb service.

Did you hear about the guy who got acupuncture?

The whole time he was on pins and needles.

What's left after the doctor has to remove part of a patient's colon?

A semicolon.

Why do mental institutions have lousy soup?

Too many kooks spoil the broth.

What's the dentist's oath?

I swear to pull the tooth, the whole tooth, and nothing but the tooth.

Why did the psychiatrist develop a split personality?

So he could see twice as many patients in a day.

Did you hear about the scientist who put laughing gas in beer?

He got brew-ha-ha.

Why did the architect's enemies cover his blueprints with Reynolds Wrap?

They wanted to foil his plans.

What type of math do they use to design aircrafts?

Plane geometry.

??????????

WHEN DOES THE MOON BURP

When it's full.

87

??????????

What do you get when scientists put the genes of a philosopher in a potato?

A potato that says, "I think, therefore I yam."

Sally: My doctor is really strange.
Last weekend, he took my appendix out.
Sue: What's so strange about that?
Sally: He took it out to dinner and a movie!

What do you call twin neurosurgeons?

A paradox.

What happens to your toes when your foot falls asleep?

They become coma-toes.

Which bone in your arm is called the humerus?

What else—the funny bone!

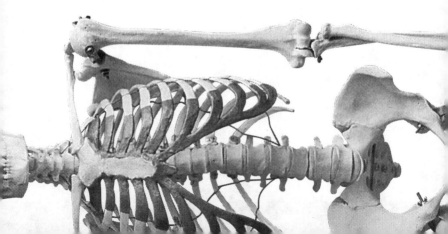

What type of team are dentists on?

The drill team.

Patient: How do the lungs work?

Doctor: Air comes in. Air goes out. I'd tell you more but I'm trying to make a lung story short.

What song do workers at a cryogenics lab sing?

"Freeze a jolly good fellow."

What vitamin is good for your eyesight?

Vitamin See.

Why did the man go to dinner with his psychiatrist?

So he could whine and dine.

89

How do you say yes to an optometrist?

Eye-eye, sir.

MONSTERS

What's the best thing about being a one-eyed Cyclops?
You can get glasses in about half an hour.

Who can be killed with a stake through the heart?
Everybody.

What's Dracula's favorite instrument to play?
The windpipe.

What kind of goblin likes blood?
A hemogoblin.

What's Dracula's favorite fruit?
An Adam's apple.

ASK JAY

HOW DO YOU KNOW THAT YOU HAVE THE RIGHT MATERIAL FOR YOUR AUDIENCE?

In order to tell a joke well, you have to be believable. For example, if you are nine years old and you are telling a joke about welding, it had better be a really funny welding joke because people are not going to believe you know what you're talking about. The more truth there is in a joke, the funnier it will be to people because they will be able to relate to it. So if you are nine years old and you are telling a joke about your parents, people will be able to identify with you and laugh along. But remember that there are certain things that other kids find funnier than adults. Any kind of bodily noise (wink, wink) kids will find hysterical and adults will say "Oh, that's horrible!" so save that kind of humor for your friends.

91

What's Dracula's favorite part of a guitar?

What else, the neck!

Why doesn't Dracula like kids?

They drive him batty.

Why is Dracula never interviewed by the press?

Because he has skeletons in his closet.

What does a lady ghost take to make her look younger?

Boo-tox.

What do you call it when a ghost scares the wrong person by mistake?

A boo-hoo.

When a vampire bites people, does it care what nationality they are?

No. As long as they're full-blooded.

What branch of the military can ghosts join?

The Ghost Guard.

What's a vampire's favorite way to travel?

On a blood vessel.

How does a female ghost dance?

She shakes her boo-ty.

Who's the most famous monster rapper?

Ghoulio.

Who's the most famous monster singer?

Christina Aghoulera.

What's a ghost's favorite magazine?
Spirits Illustrated.

**Dracula: My sister's dating
the invisible man. I don't know
what she sees in him. In fact,
he's not much to look at.**

Why don't skeletons ever get visitors?
*Because when you go to their house,
there's no body home.*

How can you tell when a ghost is rich?
He wears fitted sheets.

**Why doesn't the Wolfman ever carry
an umbrella?**
Because he's a Wash 'n' Werewolf.

**Where's Dracula's favorite place to
go waterskiing?**
Lake Eerie.

What's a ghoul's favorite snack?
Finger sandwiches.

What kinds of monsters make honey?
Zom-bees.

What kind of furniture do ghosts like?
Bam-boo!

What game do ghosts play with their babies?
Peek-a-BOO!

**What was Dr. Jekyll's favorite
game to play?**
Hyde and Go Seek.

What kind of bell is hard to hear?

A decibel.

Why is the cello the easiest instrument to make?

They use a cello mold.

Why was it a good thing that Michelangelo never celebrated Thanksgiving?

Because he was a sculptor and it would have taken him months to carve the turkey.

Why is playing Spanish guitar so easy?

Because all the music is written in the key of sí.

How does a tuba player get his tuba so shiny?

With a tuba toothpaste.

MUSIC and ART

What kind of drum can be broken, but never played?

An eardrum.

Many drummers aren't very smart.

In fact, they're often cymbal-minded.

If a truck horn goes "toot-toot," what goes "toot suite"?

A French horn.

Did you hear about the artist who did a painting of a gargoyle by the ocean?

He called it Gargoyle with Saltwater.

JERRY SEINFELD

The first time you hear the concept of Halloween when you're a kid, your brain can't even process the idea. You're like, "What is this? What did you say? Someone's giving out candy? Who's giving out candy? EVERYONE WE KNOW is just giving out candy? I gotta be a part of this!"

WOODY ALLEN

"When I was kidnapped,
my parents snapped into action.
They rented out my room."

OUTDOORS

What did the tree surgeon say about the diseased elm?

Its bark is worse than its blight.

Why is a flower dangerous?

Because it has a pistil.

What type of tree is made up of numbers and letters?

Geometry.

What kind of sand will you never find at the beach?

Ampersand.

How do you make a flower grow faster?

Just press the accelerator petal.

What color is the wind?

Blew.

What do you do if you're in the ocean and surrounded by icebergs?

Go with the floe.

Who's to blame for an earthquake?

It's the earth's fault.

What did one mushroom say to another mushroom?

When they made you, they broke the mold.

WILDEST
MISSING HOMEWORK EXCUSES

My llama ate it

Aliens abducted it

A frog hopped off with it

I did it on invisible paper

My mom fed it to my llama

I left it in a parallel universe

A gang of frogs hopped off with it

My mom fed it to a gang of alien frogs
from a parallel universe to keep them
from hopping off with my llama

Did you hear about the student who made a paper boat out of his report card because he wanted to sail the seven C's?

Something to ask your teacher:
"If I get elected president of my class, does that mean on the opening day of school, I get to throw out the first spitball?"

When is a rope like a student?

When it's taut.

When Arnold Schwarzenegger was in elementary
school, his teacher was putting on a play about
famous German composers. His teacher said,
"Arnold, since you want to be an actor,
who do you want to be in our play:
Beethoven, Brahms, or Handel?"
Little Arnold just stared at his teacher and said,
"I'll be Bach."

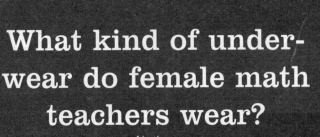

What kind of under-wear do female math teachers wear?

Algebras.

Why did the student bring his teacher a container of margarine?

He was trying to butter her up.

SCHOOL

I have no idea what "plagiarism" means.

Can I copy the answer from you?

What's the worst thing you can eat in a school cafeteria?

The food.

**What part of your body is most
like a classroom?**

Your eyes, because they have pupils.

**What do you call
someone who
studies hives?**

A B-student.

THINGS TO TELL
A SUBSTITUTE TEACHER

"Mr. Johnson never gives us homework on Wednesday.
Wednesday is coloring day."

"Mr. Johnson gives us the answers with the tests."

"The teacher's bathroom is across the street at the gas station."

"Mr. Johnson starts every day by standing on the desk and singing
'Oops! . . . I Did It Again.'"

"Mr. Johnson takes us out to lunch on Wednesday—and pays."

"The class boa constrictor is missing!"

"Mr. Johnson forbids note passing but encourages text messaging."

ASK JAY

WERE YOU GOOD IN SCHOOL?

Knowing the answer in class didn't really come easily to me. I was dyslexic, so school was never my favorite place. I was especially terrible in math. I used to put my hand up in class and ask my teacher, "Where did mathematics come from?" He would turn red. "You're not fooling anyone, Mr. Leno. Your annoying question is intended to take us off the subject; you don't care where mathematics came from!" The same teacher once wrote on my report card, "If Jay spent as much time studying as he did trying to be a comedian, he'd be a star." That confuses me to this day. How was I going to become a star without trying to be a comedian? Maybe he meant I could be some kind of a math star? No thanks.

Why are baseball stadiums never air-conditioned?

Because there are always lots of fans around.

Why are umpires so chubby?
Because they always clean their plate.

SPORTS

George Washington is famous for throwing a silver dollar across the Potomac. If he wanted to throw money away today, he'd just buy season tickets to the Clippers.

If Dracula's son played
baseball, what would he be?

Batboy.

**Why did the golfer
change his socks?**

He had a hole in one.

If athletes get
athlete's feet, what
do lifeguards get?

Undertoe.

**Where can you sue someone
for making an awful racket?**

Tennis court.

How do you know when it's cold
at Wrigley Field?

*Because the players are wearing
baseball gloves on both hands.*

What happened when the tailor
made a pair of pants from the
green felt of a pool table?

He got an eight ball in the side pocket.

Silly

QUESTIONS

What time does the eight-o'clock show start?

How long is Three Mile Island?

What's your brother like when he's alone?

Is Pope John Paul II the first pope to have that name?

ASK JAY

SHOULD YOU WATCH YOURSELF WHEN YOU PRACTICE YOUR ROUTINE?

Unless you are doing impressions, I tell people not to watch themselves. Telling jokes in front of a mirror might make you feel self-conscious. The reason a lot of actors don't make good comedians is because they do not want to be funny-looking; they want to be handsome or beautiful. But as a comedian, you want to be funny. When you are telling a story, you might distort your face in a certain way that makes people laugh. But when you practice in the mirror, you might say, "Oh, I look horrible when I do that," and stop doing what everyone thinks is funny. If you are a comedian, that should be your goal—to look funny.

Wooden windows wobbled when Wednesday's wicked westerly winds were wailing.

Always give the bratwurst to the worst brat.

I purchased pretty poor pith helmets on the path to Perth.

Sean, Sam, and Sarah should see the seashells I saw in the Seychelles.

Seven spunky skunks slyly skied sideways since six sorry sparrows skied straight.

How much ground could a groundhog hog if a groundhog could hog ground?

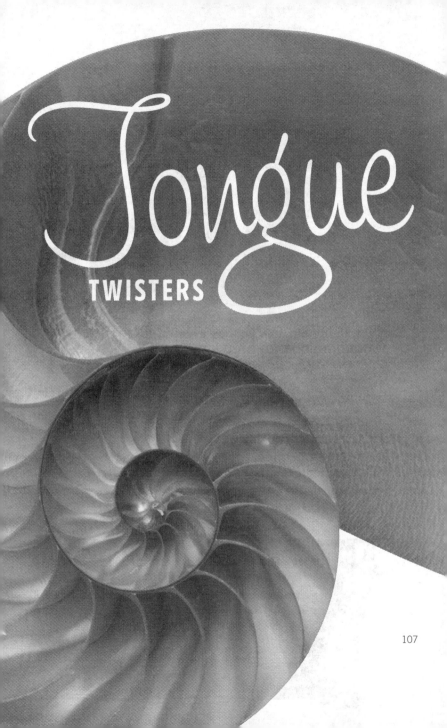

Tongue
TWISTERS

What kind of saw do you use to cut driftwood?

A seasaw.

Can you figure out this holiday greeting?
ABCDEFGHIJKMNOPQRSTUVWXYZ.

Answer: No L—Noel.

What do you call an Indian who doesn't laugh much?

Minnehaha.

Tina: My grandfather had a store that stood in the same spot for fifty years.

Lena: Must have been a stationery store.

GOOFIEST DINOSAUR NAMES

Albertosaurus ★ Baryonyx ★ Psittacosaurus ★ Diplodocus ★
Kentrosaurus ★ Gryposaurus ★ Quetzalcoatlus ★
Compsognathus ★ Hypacrosaurus ★
Rhamphorhynchus ★ Muttaburrasaurus ★
Massospondylus ★ Ichthyosaurus ★
Lambeosaurus ★ Ultrasaurus ★ Heterodontosaurus ★
Tuojiangosaurus ★ Saltasaurus ★

What are a pirate's two favorite letters of the alphabet?

C and Arrrrrrrr!

Cky

wordplay

Are palm trees always green?

Yes. Except at a fortune teller's, where palms are red.

A Hindu husband and wife were discussing what they would like to come back as in the next life, if they could come back as anything at all.

He said, "I would like to come back as a bank vault because then I would be rich."

She said, "I would like to come back as a dress so then I would be beautiful."

"I'm afraid that my choice is better," said the husband.

"Why do you say that?" asked his wife.

"Because it is always better to be safe than sari."

What did the nut say to the screw?

"Let's bolt."

What detergent is best for washing Christmas stockings?

Yule Tide.

Did you hear about the playwright with the broken leg?

He was so mad at the actors in his play that he cast his entire cast at the entire cast.

Did you hear about the paperboy who was fired?

When it came to throwing the daily paper, he did it weakly.

What's the tip of the iceberg?

15 to 20 percent of the iceberg's bill.

If you put an income tax on income and a property tax on property, what kind of tax do you put on chairs?

Thumbtacks!

What's a rapper's favorite playground game?

Hip-hopscotch.

What's the difference between a small vacuum cleaner and a cleaning lady in a museum?

One is a DustBuster and the other is a bust duster.

Why did the
BOX

He wanted to hit the books.

E R ?

go to the library

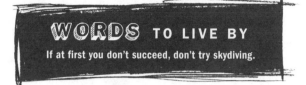

How does a rapper's telephone ring?

Bling-bling.

114

Did you hear about the tree trimmer who wanted to be in show business?

Every time he took a bough, he took a bow.

Why did the man carry a mattress around on his back?

He always wanted to have something

to fall back on.

Why did the farmer spend hours talking to his cornfield?

Because they were all ears.

Why did the girl go to sea?

She wanted to meet some buoys.

How can you tell if a kid is rich?

When she keeps her money in a Swiss piggy bank.

What do you say to a sailor who's been on land for years?

Long time no sea.

Why are contortionists the nicest people on earth?
Because they'll bend over backward for you.

How many lawyers does it take to screw in a lightbulb?
Two. One to screw it in and another to file a personal injury lawsuit.

Which is longer—60 minutes or 48 hours?
They're both an hour long on CBS.

What does the following tell you about Billy:
APPRECIATED
BILLY
WEIGHT
Billy is overweight and underappreciated.

What union do mimes belong to?
The United Mime Workers.

Why did the airline pilot get fired?
He took off too many days.

How can you touch your right eyebrow and your left eyebrow at the same time with only one finger?
If you do it while looking in a mirror.

What's the name of this piece of clothing: 22.
A tutu.

What do you get when two really overweight guys stand in the rain for a long time?
Saturated fats.

What do you call a

MOUN

that boxes?

TAIN

119

Rocky.

How do you turn adobe into a home?

Exchange the letters d and b in it, so you have "abode."

And now the five-day forecast: Monday to be followed by Tuesday, Wednesday, Thursday, and Friday.

Why don't you ever see dandruff on a man wearing a toupee?

Because he sweeps it under the rug.

Who drew the plans for Noah's Ark?

An ark-itect.

How do you hang up an airplane?

On an airplane hanger!

What's an undertaker's favorite time of day?

Mourning.

Which conjunction do you need in a rowboat?

An or.

What did the policeman say to the mime he was arresting?

"You have the right to remain silent."

What's the difference between a sailor and a fat guy?

A sailor gets stuck on a desert isle but a fat guy gets stuck in the dessert aisle.

PERFECT PUT-DOWNS

cheese breath ★ Brillo head ★
Sasquatch ★ peanut head ★
sausage fingers ★ chowhound ★
troglodyte ★ chowderhead

WHAT
DO YOU CALL
SOMEONE
WHOSE NAME WAS ONCE
LEE?

Formerly.

ASK JAY

HAS BEING A COMEDIAN HELPED YOU IN OTHER ASPECTS OF YOUR LIFE?

Humor can help you deal with a lot of situations. Where another person may get mad and punch someone in the face, you can break that tension with jokes. You can't stay angry if you are laughing. Also, all of the things that make you different from your classmates, anything you've ever been picked on for or teased about, can be the basis of your best jokes. Your life will be easier when you realize you don't necessarily want to be like everyone else.

How did the cowboy ride a horse across a river that was thirty feet deep?

He put the horse in a boat and rowed it across.

A man was summoned to the court of the king and was dumbfounded to see that His Majesty was only a foot high.

"Stop staring," the king said to him.

"Haven't you ever heard of a twelve-inch ruler?"

What do bullfighters use on their skin?

Oil of Olé.

A rock and a stone wanted to ask a pebble out on a date. Who finally did it?

The rock, because it was a little boulder.

What do you call a gorilla who plays golf?

Hairy Putter.

Which airline do rich people fly?

Billion Air.

What's a cowboy's favorite Web site?

Yahoo!

What's the name of this town:
AND
MASS

Andover, Mass.

Did you hear about the pirate who made a sword out of meat?

It was a veal cutlass.

Some cannibals captured a fortune teller and were discussing the best way to cook her. One said, "I think I'd like her well done."

To which the chief replied,

"It's rare that a medium is well done."

What did the small desk lamp say when it was out on the street asking for money?

"Can you spare some change? I'm a little light."

What kind of phone can be heard, but not talked into?

A xylophone.

What did the mop say to the bucket?

"Are you okay? You look a little pail."

How does a British policeman keep his badge on?

With a bobby pin.

WHAT Did You SAY ???

Store Clerk: May I help you?
Shoplifter: No thanks, I'm helping myself.

Farmer #1: My horse can count to five by stomping on the ground.
Farmer #2: That's nothing. I've got a pair of rabbits that can multiply.

Girl #1: When I was in the hospital last week I think the doctor was hitting on me.
Girl #2: Hitting on you? Why do you say that?
Girl #1: Because when he examined me he said I had a cute appendicitis.

Girl: Have you ever been to Seattle?
Guy: I sure have.
Girl: What's Puget Sound like?
Guy: I don't know. I never heard it.

Bill: Every time I'm with Susan, she drives me up a wall.

Ted: You mean she's that annoying?

Bill: No, I mean she's that bad a driver.

Man #1: How much of the newspaper do you read every day?

Man #2: Just the ground floor.

Man #1: The ground floor?

Man #2: Yeah. I never get past the first story.

Man: Why does your pony's whinny sound so funny?

Farmer: Because he's a little hoarse.

Guy: The Pilgrims were a very nonviolent people. That's why they wore buckles on their shoes.

Girl: What do buckles on their shoes have to do with being nonviolent?

Guy: It was so no one would hit them below the belt.

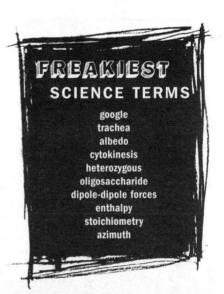

FREAKIEST
SCIENCE TERMS

google
trachea
albedo
cytokinesis
heterozygous
oligosaccharide
dipole-dipole forces
enthalpy
stoichiometry
azimuth

ASK JAY

DID YOUR FAMILY ENCOURAGE YOU TO BE A COMEDIAN?

My mother always told me there was a time to be funny and a time to be serious. According to her, the time to be funny was approximately never. I could be joking around on a ride at Disneyland and my mother would say, "Not here." Even after I got reasonably famous my mother would tell me, "Now Jay, no one likes someone who tells jokes *all* the time. Why don't you do a little dance or sing a little song and then tell a joke." That was my mother's show business advice: "No one wants to hear jokes all the time!" Thanks, Ma.

Guy: I've got to get rid of this palm tree.

Girl: Be sure to give it a frond farewell.

BILL COSBY

As I have discovered by examining my past, I started out as a child. Coincidentally, so did my brother. My mother did not put all her eggs in one basket, so to speak: She gave me a younger brother named Russell, who taught me what was meant by survival of the fittest.

ELLEN DEGENERES

People always ask me, "Were you funny as a child?" Well, no, I was an accountant.

RODNEY DANGERFIELD

I had plenty of pimples as a kid. One day I fell asleep in the library. When I woke up, a blind man was reading my face.

CHRIS ROCK

Charlie Brown is the one person I identify with. Charlie Brown is such a loser. He wasn't even the star of his own Halloween special.

JIM CARREY

Green Eggs and Ham was the story of my life. I wouldn't eat a thing when I was a kid, but Dr. Seuss inspired me to try cauliflower.

Man: Do your cows get milked in the barn?
Farmer: No, we milk them in the udder place.

Girl: They say that Superman fights for "Truth, Justice, and the American Way." What's the American way?
Guy: These days? About 220 pounds.

Girl: You know if you eat really slowly, you won't gain weight.
Guy: I never heard that.
Girl: Sure. Haste makes waist.

Girl: Did you hear that lobsters celebrate Christmas?
Guy: How do you know that?
Girl: Because they have Sandy Claws.

WORDS
THAT SOUND LIKE INSULTS BUT AREN'T

dogmatic bugaboo spelunker
masticator pyranose crumhorn
scabbard kookaburra garibaldi
gumwood microlith Vegemite

Nurse: Do you know what your blood type is?
Patient: I think it's red.

Bill: Do you think that eating red meat is bad for you?
Phil: It's not as bad as eating green meat. I ate some that I found in my refrigerator the other day. Boy, was I sick.

Ava: My uncle's a masseur, but he likes to sing all day long.
Nicky: Really? What's he sing?
Ava: "People . . . people who knead people."

John: I just wrote a kids' book about a tugboat that was arrested for robbing a bank.
Susie: What happens to him?
John: He's tried by a jury of his piers.

Gina: What's your ideal weight?
Tina: Five to ten minutes. Then I leave.

Drew: My brother's starting to lose his hair, so I'm giving him some of mine.
Dan: Why are you doing that?
Drew: Because it's better to give than to recede.

Sandy: My brother's in trouble with the humane society.
Mandy: Why?
Sandy: He put harnesses on all the cats and dogs in the neighborhood.
Mandy: What in the world did he do that for?
Sandy: To rein cats and dogs.

Justin: Do you believe in animal rights?
Julie: No. I've never seen any animal that writes.

Mike: Why is Tommy standing in the kitchen pantry wearing a red suit with the number 57 on his chest?
Matt: He's playing ketchup.

Mary: **Why did you nominate Jason for president of the club?**

Peter: I think he'd be good at it.

Mary: **But he's just the secretary. All he does is write. He's not a leader!**

Peter: He has lead pencils.

Dawn: My father just became an organ donor.
Dan: Really, what organ did he donate?
Dawn: His Wurlitzer.

Deb: How was your Thanksgiving?
Jack: Terrible. I got grounded.
Deb: What happened?
Jack: My mom was making the turkey and I told her to "go stuff it."

Jeff: I hate playing pool with Wayne. Before every game, he insists on rubbing the top of the table with his hands.
Larry: He's just playing by the rule.
Jeff: What rule?
Larry: The rule that says the top of a regulation pool table must be felt.

Jacques: I would like you to take a look at my aquarium.
Gino: What can I do about it? I'm only a shoemaker.
Jacques: Well, I thought you could give me new eels and soles.

Man: What's the last letter in the dictionary?

Girl: Z.

Man: No, DICTIONARY ends in Y.

Customer: The second hand is missing from this watch. Can you fix it?

Jeweler: Sorry, can't fix it here.
You have to go to a secondhand store.

Guy: Marc Antony must have really liked corn.

Girl: Why do you say that?

Guy: Because he said, "Friends, Romans, and countrymen, lend me your ears."

Reporter: Have you found the Abominable Snowman?

Scientist: Not yeti.

Girl: Your hair's all messed up. Why don't you comb it?

Guy: I don't own a comb. It's too much trouble.

Girl: How is owning a comb too much trouble?

Guy: Didn't you ever hear the saying, "A man's comb is his hassle?"

FUNNY
PEOPLE IN HISTORY

ABRAHAM LINCOLN
Asked about his experience as a soldier, replied that he'd had "a good many bloody struggles with mosquitoes."

BENJAMIN FRANKLIN
"Guests, like fish, begin to smell after three days."

ALBERT EINSTEIN
"Once you can accept the universe as matter expanding into nothing that is something, wearing stripes with plaid comes easy."

GOLDA MEIR
"Moses took us Israelis forty years through the desert in order to bring us to the one spot in the Middle East that has no oil!"

THEODORE ROOSEVELT
After reading a scathing review of a book he wrote, sent the critic a note reading, "I regret to state that my family and intimate friends are delighted with your review of my book."

ARISTOTLE
"The gods too are fond of a joke."

WINSTON CHURCHILL
"When I am abroad, I always make it a rule never to criticize or attack the government of my country. I make up for lost time when I am at home."

MARGARET THATCHER
"In politics, if you want anything said, ask a man; if you want anything done, ask a woman."

MAHATMA GANDHI
"I believe in equality for everyone, except reporters and photographers."

NAPOLÉON BONAPARTE
"Never interrupt your enemy when he is making a mistake."

DANIEL BOONE
"I have never been lost, but I will admit to being confused for several weeks."